Supercharged Productivity

Maximizing Mental Energy and Focus

Table of Contents

Chapter 1. Introduction

Get ready to supercharge your life with our Special Report titled "Supercharged Productivity: Maximizing Mental Energy and Focus". Dive into a sea of innovative strategies that promise to not only boost your mental stamina but also give you laser-like focus to conquer any task. This is not some high-end technical manuscript, but a friendly guidebook filled with accessible, practical, and potent methods that are bound to revolutionize your day-to-day productivity. Find out how you can tap into your brain's hidden potential and transform standard workdays into extraordinary ones. Get ready to overcome your productivity hurdles and step into a world where peak performance is not a sporadic occurrence, but your new norm! So, buckle up and prepare for the ride of a lifetime towards maximized efficiency and success with our Special Report!

Chapter 2. Unleashing Your Mental Energy: The Basics

In our quest for supercharged productivity, it's vital we start with understanding the foundation upon which all our mental processes are built. This foundation is often overlooked in many sources, yet it's crucial to achieving the heightened cognition we seek. So, what is this foundation I hear you ask? It is your mental energy—the fuel of the brain. Once you learn how to tap into this powerful resource, you'll be amazed at what you can accomplish.

Before we delve into how to unleash this energy, it's crucial we understand what exactly it is, what can diminish it, and how to replenish it. Let's begin with its basic definition.

Mental energy, or cognitive energy, can be defined as the energy used by the brain for cognitive tasks including (but not limited to) learning, memory, and problem-solving. Just like a car needs gas to function, your brain requires mental energy to carry out these tasks effectively.

2.1. Understanding Brain Energy Consumption

The brain, weighing just about 2% of your total body weight, astoundingly, uses up to 20% of your body's total energy budget. A considerable part of this energy is used in "housekeeping" functions to maintain cell health, and for cycling of neurotransmitters, or communication molecules. Neurons, the brain cells responsible for transmitting information, are excessively energetic, and it's their high energy need that contributes significantly to the brain's overall energy consumption. To simplify, mental energy is the fuel needed by these neurons to transmit information efficiently.

However, the brain's energy reserve is finite. After prolonged cognitive tasks such as studying, working on a project, or even engaging in intense conversation, you might find your concentration waning, and mental fatigue setting in. This is a result of your brain depleting its energy supplies. Understanding how to prevent such depletion, or replenishing mental energy once it's low, becomes crucial in our pursuit of peak performance.

2.2. Causes of Mental Energy Drain

Several factors can drain your mental energy without you realizing it until it's too late. Some common culprits include:

- **Lack of Sleep:** Our brain regenerates during deep sleep through a process called glymphatic clearance, removing waste products that can impair cognitive function if not properly disposed of. That explains why we feel refreshed and mentally sharp after a good night's rest. Deprive your brain of quality sleep, and it's akin to running a marathon with a backpack full of rocks.

- **Poor Nutrition:** Our brains are powered by glucose. A lack of proper nutrients, or consuming too much sugar and processed foods, can cause glucose levels to swing, leading to mental energy highs and crashes. Your meals should consist of balanced quantities of proteins, good fats, and complex carbohydrates for sustained energy.

- **Chronic Stress:** Stress triggers the release of cortisol, our primary stress hormone, which over the long term, can suppress brain function, impacting creativity, memory, and problem-solving abilities.

Being aware of these factors allows us to prevent unnecessary brain energy expenditure and hence, preserve more for demanding cognitive tasks.

2.3. Boosting Mental Energy Utilization

There are several ways to boost your brain's energy utilization. Here are a few starting points:

- **Hydrate:** Dehydration results in a loss in focus, and impairs short-term memory. So, ensure you take regular sips of water throughout your workday.

- **Healthy Snacks:** Include snacks rich in omega-3s, like seeds and nuts, or fresh fruits to keep your energy levels stable.

- **Active Breaks:** Simple exercises like stretching or quick walks help with blood circulation, delivering oxygen and nutrients to your brain, making you more alert.

- **Mindfulness:** Techniques such as meditation can help de-stress and enhance concentration. Even a few minutes daily can result in significant improvements.

2.4. Harnessing Your Mental Energy

Harnessing our brain's energy effectively is what differentiates the super productive from the average. Here are some strategies:

- **Pomodoro Technique:** This time-management method advocates for 25-minute focused work sessions, punctuated by short breaks. This is in line with our brain's natural ability to concentrate on a single task before mental fatigue sets in.

- **Single-Tasking:** Multitasking is the enemy of mental energy. Focusing on one task at a time preserves and prioritizes your mental energy.

- **Positive Energy Management:** Dwell on positive thoughts and positive experiences to build your mental energy reservoir.

Although these might sound simplistic, their cumulative impact on mental energy and focus is substantial. Bottom-line—our brains have a fantastic capacity to function incredibly if they're well-fueled.

By understanding the basic concepts of managing mental energy, you will notice a substantial shift in the quality of your output. You will start to experience fewer mental blocks, work through responsibilities with relative ease, and accomplish more in less time. The effects of unleashing your mental energy are not confined to your work life alone; they pervade every facet of the personal territories as well. So, it's about time to get started, unleash the power within, and supercharge your life!

Chapter 3. Understanding Focus: A Comprehensive Overview

If you've ever tried to concentrate on a task, you've no doubt experienced the delight of being completely immersed in the moment. Your attention is laser-focused, you're in 'the zone,' and productivity is at an all-time high. Other times, however, staying focused is akin to taming the wild wind. In the fluctuating sea of concentration, understanding the nuances of focus becomes paramount.

3.1. The Science behind Focus

Focus refers to the cognitive mechanism that allows us to zero in on relevant information and tasks while excluding irrelevant distractions. Substantiated by neuroscience, focus operates on the principle of 'selective attention.' Certain regions of our brain, including the prefrontal and parietal cortex, put attention to work, allowing us to engage in goal-directed actions.

Our prefrontal cortex, the brain's executive control center, ensures we stay on task, while the parietal cortex aids in shifting attention. Working together, these spatially distributed networks orchestrate our attentional focus.

3.2. Types of Focus

Understanding focus requires a grasp of its various forms, namely voluntary and involuntary focus. Voluntary focus, also known as Endogenous Attention, involves consciously directing our minds towards a task. Problem-solving and active learning necessitate this type of attentive engagement.

Involuntary focus, or Exogenous Attention, is driven by external stimuli that catch our attention. These attention-grabbers can either aid our focus or serve as distractions, depending on their relevance to our task at hand.

3.3. Factors that Influence Focus

A multitude of external and internal factors influences our focus and attention. Environmental disruptions, like unexpected noise or visual stimuli, can attract our Exogenous Attention and sidetrack us from our tasks. Internal states such as stress, anxiety, fatigue, and even hunger can impair our ability to maintain sustained focus.

Moreover, our emotional state can dictate our level of concentration. When emotions run high, our focus can become divided, making concerted attention more challenging.

3.4. The Role of Focus in Productivity

Sharper focus equals heightened productivity - this principle underscores the relevance of focus in our daily lives. The ability to concentrate on tasks without being side-tracked boosts efficiency, enhances problem-solving capabilities, and breeds innovation. Lack of focus, on the other hand, significantly lowers productivity, strains our cognitive resources, and, over time, leads to mental exhaustion.

3.5. Enhancing Your Focus

Our focus, though not always within our immediate control, can certainly be honed and enhanced. Attention-based exercises, mindfulness practices, and deliberate mental breaks are proven to facilitate focus. Regular physical activity is beneficial too, as it stimulates brain health, improves mood, and reduces stress.

Deep work techniques, such as time-blocking where you dedicate specific time pockets for high-focus tasks, can be advantageous. Coupling these practices with effective workspace organization will minimize distractions and facilitate an environment conducive to focus.

3.6. Understanding Distractions

Despite our best intentions, distractions abound. These attention-grabbers can manifest as environmental noise, a bombardment of digital notifications, or even our wandering minds. Analyzing the nature of our distractions can help us devise strategies to combat them effectively.

While strategies to tackle external distractions include creating a distraction-free workspace, coping with internal distractions can be more complex. Monotasking, mindfulness, and cognitive behavioral techniques can help deal with mental clutter and sustain focus.

3.7. Embracing the Power of Rest

Understand that focus, like any other cognitive resource, is finite. Recognizing and respecting your attentional limits ensures sustainable productivity in the long run. Incorporating adequate rest and breaks into your work schedule can prevent cognitive fatigue, recharge your focus, and enhance mental stamina over time.

3.8. Focus and Mental Wellness

Beyond productivity and efficiency, focus impacts our mental wellbeing. Feeling perpetually distracted can breed feelings of guilt, anxiety, and frustration, taking a toll on our mental health in the long run. On the flip side, achieving a state of focus can foster a sense of accomplishment and wellbeing. Similarly, practices that improve focus, such as mindfulness and exercise, yield tangible mental health benefits too.

In essence, understanding focus means comprehending the factors that affect it, mechanisms underlying it, and strategies to harness it. As you dive deeper into this vast ocean of cognitive functioning, you will not only get closer to supercharging your productivity but also realize how focus influences the overarching quality of your life. Fully grasping this understanding may be challenging, but it'd be a delightful venture worth the effort.

Armed with this knowledge, you can now go forth and explore the tactical approaches we'll discuss next to supercharge your focus and by extension, your productivity. Now, isn't that a goal worth pursuing?

Chapter 4. The Science of Productivity: What Really Works

In this age where hustling is considered a virtue, productivity has become a key buzzword, and finding ways to increase it is one of the most sought-after pursuits. What if we tell you the secret to productivity is rooted in science? Indeed, understanding why we work the way we do can provide crucial insights into how we can work better.

4.1. The Problem with the 8-Hour Workday

The 8-hour workday has become the standard for modern work. However, this concept originated during the Industrial Revolution when productivity was measured by the quantity of physical labor, not intellectual creativity or problem-solving skills. In our present-day knowledge-based economy, the mental energy we expend cannot be bound by a one-size-fits-all 8-hour workday standard.

According to research, the human brain can only focus for about 90 to 120 minutes before needing a break. This principle, called Ultradian Rhythms, forms the basis for the Pomodoro Technique, wherein periods of focused work are alternated with short breaks.

The takeaway here is to divide your workday into 'work bursts' of approximately 90 minutes, followed by 15-minute breaks. This way, we align our working pattern with our brain's natural energy fluctuations, thereby minimizing burnout and enhancing productivity.

4.2. The Power of Deep Work

Introduced by Georgetown University Professor Cal Newport, the concept of deep work involves eliminating all distractions and focusing intensely on a cognitive task. This level of concentration harnesses the brain's full potential and leads to high productivity.

However, deep work isn't just about working hard; it's about working smart. It means strategically scheduling your work, knowing when your brain is most active, and using that time to perform complex tasks.

Moreover, it's important to remember that like muscles, our brain capacity isn't infinite. Fatigue can set in with overuse, leading to decreased productivity. Therefore, make sure you intersperse periods of deep work with rest.

4.3. Understanding The Role of Energy Cycles

One size doesn't fit all — this applies equally well to energy cycles and productivity. Every individual operates on a unique biological clock, or Circadian Rhythm, which determines their stamina and attention peaks and troughs. Notably, these rhythms can generally categorize people into morning larks, night owls, or intermediate types. Aligning work schedules with your Circadian Rhythms can greatly enhance productivity.

A closely related concept is Chronotypes. It refers to the predispositions of individuals towards alertness at certain times. Understanding your Chronotype can help you optimize your work hours and also schedule tasks aptly - creative tasks when your energy level is high, and admin-related work during the lower energy period.

4.4. The Significance of Minimalism for Productivity

Minimalism isn't about owning less but possessing only what serves a purpose. When applied to productivity, minimalism is all about reducing cognitive load. It means finding the most efficient way to complete tasks and avoiding unnecessary steps that might lead to decision fatigue.

While undertaking a task, if one is overwhelmed with too much information or too many tasks, they are likely to be slow in making decisions or fail to make one at all. The solution to this is the concept of single-tasking, focusing on one task at a time instead of juggling multiple assignments. Paring down to the essentials also means using simpler, more effective tools to manage tasks and timelines. This can significantly enhance your efficiency and output.

4.5. Emphasizing The Role of Rest in Productivity

When really busy, one often overlooks or intentionally skips the downtime. However, rest and relaxation are critical elements to productivity. It's during relaxation periods that the brain engages with the 'Default Mode Network,' which enhances creativity and problem-solving abilities.

Moreover, sleep plays a crucial role in our cognitive functions. A lack of it can lead to decreased concentration, memory, and learning skills. It's not just about a straight 8-hour sleep; napping has also been shown to enhance productivity. A study by NASA on sleepy military pilots and astronauts found that a 40-minute nap improved performance by 34% and alertness by 100%.

4.6. The Influence of Physical Activity on Productivity

Physical exercise isn't just good for the body but also for the brain. According to a Harvard Business Review, regular exercise brings about improvements in time management, mental performance, mood, and boosted creativity.

The release of energy during physical activity enables better concentration and focus on tasks. A simple incorporation of exercises in your daily routine, such as walking meetings, taking stairs instead of elevators, or short workout breaks, can provide the necessary boosts of energy and productivity.

4.7. Tapping Into The Cognitive Benefits of Nutrition

The brain consumes nearly 20-30% of our daily calories. Therefore, food significantly influences our brain health and productivity. Certain nutrients, like omega-3 fatty acids (found in fish and nuts), antioxidants (in fruits and vegetables), and B-vitamins (in whole grains, meat, and dairy products), are known to boost brain health. Additionally, keeping yourself hydrated also helps maintain high mental performance.

4.8. The Key Role of Mindfulness and Meditation

Several studies support the idea that mindfulness and meditation can improve focus, cognitive flexibility, relationship satisfaction, and mental health while reducing stress and anxiety. Activities promoting mindfulness, such as journaling, meditation, yoga, or simply being present in the moment, help clear mental clutter. This leads to improved concentration and productivity.

In conclusion, productivity is a jigsaw puzzle made up of several components – working in alignment with your energy cycles, practicing deep work, embracing minimalism, allowing time for relaxation, regular physical exercise, maintaining a healthy diet, and nurturing mindfulness. Everyone may have a unique way of piecing this puzzle together, but understanding the underlying science aids in creating your optimal productivity path. Embrace these strategies, tailor them to your lifestyle, and watch your productivity soar to new heights.

Chapter 5. Fueling the Brain: Nutrition and Mental Energy

Let's begin by appreciating the astounding complexity of the brain. With more than 85 billion neurons and nearly one quadrillion connections, it is an intricate powerhouse incessantly drawing on energy reserves to undertake functions ranging from basic survival to cognitive processes such as thinking and dreaming. Despite making up approximately 2% of our body's total weight, the brain is responsible for consuming a staggering 20% of our energy intake.

Given its high-energy demand, the way we feed our brains can significantly impact its function. The right nutrients and foods will amplify cognitive functions such as memory, creativity, and concentration, while poor dietary habits can contribute to mental fatigue, decreased mental agility, and neurological disorders.

5.1. Essential Nutrients for Optimum Brain Function

Before delving into specific foods and diet principles to fuel your brain, it's essential to understand the key nutrients your brain needs for optimal performance.

First, let's consider glucose. The main fuel for your brain is glucose, derived predominantly from carbohydrates in your diet. When your glucose levels are stable, you'll likely experience improved concentration and memory. Conversely, low glucose levels can lead to cognitive problems including poor memory and difficulty concentrating. Consuming slow-release, complex carbohydrates will ensure a steady supply of glucose to your brain.

Secondly, the brain's cellular structure is largely made up of fats, mainly in the form of omega-3 and omega-6 essential fatty acids. These help form cell membranes, support neuron function, and are involved in the synthesis of neurotransmitters.

In addition to fats and glucose, the brain requires an array of vitamins and minerals to function optimally. B vitamins are pivotal in the synthesis of neurotransmitters and the production of energy, while minerals such as iron, iodine, and zinc are essential for brain development and function.

5.2. The Brain-Boosting Diet

In order to fuel your brain, you'll need to incorporate a variety of nutrient-dense foods in your diet that will provide the essential elements we just discussed. This section will outline some of the best foods to include in a brain-boosting diet.

1. Whole Grains: Whole grains like brown rice, oats, and quinoa provide a stable source of energy for the brain due to their low-glycemic index, which ensures a slow release of glucose into the bloodstream.

2. Fatty Fish: Rich in omega-3 fatty acids, fatty fish like salmon, mackerel, and tuna support brain health. Omega-3s are essential for brain function and can slow age-related mental decline and help ward off Alzheimer's disease.

3. Leafy Greens: Broccoli, kale, spinach, and other leafy greens are rich in antioxidants and vitamin K, which supports brain health. They also contain lutein, a compound that researchers think might stave off cognitive decline.

4. Eggs: These are a great source of several nutrients tied to brain health, including vitamins B6 and B12, folate, and choline. Choline is used by the body to produce acetylcholine, which assists in regulating mood and memory.

5. Nuts and Seeds: These are also excellent sources of antioxidants,

and both have been linked to improved heart health. Since the heart and brain are closely linked, factors that impact your heart can also promote brain health.

6. Berries: Colourful and delicious, berries are packed with antioxidants that delay brain aging and improve memory.

5.3. Optimizing Meals for Cognitive Support

Incorporating these nutrient-dense foods into your daily meals can offer continuous support for your cognitive functions. Here's a daily meal plan to kickstart your brain-boosting diet.

Breakfast: Start your day with a nutrient-packed smoothie. Mix together spinach, avocado, blueberries, and Greek yogurt for a hefty dose of vitamins, fats, and proteins.

Lunch: Opt for a healthful salad comprising leafy greens, topped with grilled salmon and sprinkled with chia seeds. This will provide proteins, omega-3 fatty acids, and a wealth of essential vitamins.

Dinner: How about a bowl of lentil soup with a side of quinoa salad for dinner? It provides a good mix of slow-releasing carbohydrates, essential proteins, fiber, and a plethora of vitamins.

5.4. Smart Supplementation

While maintaining a nutrient-dense, balanced diet should always be the first line of action, adding smart supplementation can further enhance your cognitive function. Several dietary supplements have been discovered to offer potent neuroprotective benefits.

B Vitamins: Recognized for their role in brain health, especially B6, folate (B9), and B12, they protect against homocysteine build-up, which can lead to neurological disorders.

Omega-3 Fatty Acids: This supplement ensures adequate fatty acids, particularly beneficial if you are unable to consume seafood regularly.

Curcumin: The primary active component in turmeric, curcumin possesses powerful antioxidant and anti-inflammatory benefits that boost brain health.

We have essentially boarded the nutrition train to enhanced mental energy. Equipped with this understanding of what nutrients serve your brain and which foods can provide those powerhouses, you can curate a personalized food plan to suit your lifestyle and preferences. Paired with strategic supplementation, you're bound to experience the difference in your cognitive abilities.

Remember, what works best for you may not work as well for others and vice versa. Practice intuitive eating, paying attention to how different foods affect your mind and body. Fuelling your brain doesn't just involve feeding it but also understanding and respecting its unique needs and reactions. Happy mindful eating!

Chapter 6. Exercise and Mental Stamina: The Undeniable Link

Interest in the relationship between exercise and mental stamina has surged over the last few years in both scientific research and popular culture, and for a good reason. The link between physical activity and cognitive prowess is not just striking - it's undeniable. The age-old adage 'healthy mind in a healthy body' holds firm because medical science has demonstrated that regular physical exercise promotes a range of neurophysiological benefits that can improve our mental stamina and, ultimately, supercharge productivity.

6.1. Understanding Mental Stamina

Mental stamina is a measure of your ability to focus on a task without becoming mentally exhausted. It plays a critical role in maintaining high productivity levels. Mental stamina helps you push through distractions, overcome obstacles, resist fatigue and ultimately boosts cognition, memory, and intellectual prowess.

Here is where regular physical exercise comes in. The link between exercise and mental stamina lies in the physiological changes that occur in your body when you work out, all of which greatly affect your brain.

6.2. How Exercise Affects the Brain

Physical exercise triggers a cascade of responses in the body, and more crucially, in the brain. Physical activity leads to the production of a protein in the brain called Brain-Derived Neurotrophic Factor (BDNF). BDNF promotes the growth and survival of many neuronal cells, acting like fertilizer for the brain. Regular workouts contribute to higher levels of this 'miracle-gro,' enhancing your cognitive abilities and mental stamina.

The primary benefits of exercise on brain function are:

1. Improved Cognition: Exercise increases blood flow to the brain. This increased cerebral blood flow brings more oxygen and nutrients that are essential for heightened brain function.

2. Enhanced Memory: Regular exercise increases the volume of the hippocampus - the part of the brain responsible for memory and learning. This structural enhancement improves memory and prevents cognitive decline.

3. Stress Relief: Exercise decreases the body's stress hormones like cortisol and increases the production of endorphins- chemicals in the brain that act as natural painkillers and mood elevators.

6.3. The Cognitive-Boosting Workout Plan

A randomized controlled trial found that moderate-intensity exercise led to neurophysiological changes that improved cognitive function and increased mental stamina. However, you might wonder what kind of exercise leads to these benefits and how much you should do.

The answer is in incorporating three main forms of exercise: 1. Cardiovascular Exercise 2. Strength Training 3. Flexibility and Balance Exercises

Regular cardiovascular exercise like running, swimming, or biking contributes to increased heart rate, which pumps more oxygen to the brain. Strength training exercises such as weight lifting or resistance training produce distinct benefits in the brain and improve overall cognitive function. Flexibility and balance exercises like yoga or

Pilates can help relax your mind and increase your ability to focus.

For maximizing the impact of your workout on cognitive function, scientists suggest 150 minutes of moderate to vigorous physical activity spread throughout a week, or on average, 30 minutes per day for five days a week.

6.4. Tips to Incorporate Exercise Into Your Routine

Balancing exercise with a busy schedule might seem overwhelming at first. Here are some tips to help you begin:

1. Start Small: If you are not in the habit of exercising regularly, it's best to start small. Any physical activity is better than none.

2. Find Activities You Enjoy: You're more likely to continue exercising if you choose activities that you find fun and enjoyable. This will help ensure consistency.

3. Use Active Forms of Transportation: Walk or cycle to work or use the stairs instead of the elevator.

4. Try Active Meetings: Try walking meetings, or take a walk while on a call.

6.5. Conclusion

The link between exercise and mental stamina is undeniable. Regular workouts not only make you physically healthier, but they also contribute to sharper mental stamina. The investment of a small chunk of your day into exercising can pay off with an immense return in productivity. So, why not lace up your sneakers and hit the gym, take that yoga class or go for a run around the block? The benefits for your brain, your productivity, and your overall health are entirely worth it.

Chapter 7. Mastering Time Management: Essential Strategies

The realization dawns universally on us all that a single invaluable resource in life is time. While it seems to extend infinitely before us, each second spent ticking away can never be reclaimed. The crux of achieving your goals, managing your day, and ultimately running your life smoothly lies in a single concept, i.e., time management.

The efficient utilization of this twenty-four-hour resource that we each have in a day is a skillset everyone can massively benefit from. When we master time management, we not only make our days more productive but also reduce stress and live better, happier lives.

7.1. The Philosophy of Time

Understanding time as a concept and its importance in our lives is the first step towards mastering time management. Time is often equated to money, but arguably it's infinitely more valuable; money, lost, can be regained, while time, once passed, is gone forever. This fundamental truth should underline your approach to time management.

Value your hours and minutes as you would your hard-earned money. Better yet, evaluate the loss of time in terms of a potential financial loss, not to create anxiety, but to establish an understanding of time as a valuable asset.

7.2. Building Your Time Management Toolkit

As with any craft, mastering time management requires a set of appropriate tools. It includes both physical tools like calendars, task lists, time trackers, productivity apps and the mental ones, such as the ability to prioritize, plan, delegate, and say no. Let's look at each of these crucial components individually.

1. **Calendars**: Your calendar is your roadmap. It should include all essential appointments and deadlines but be flexible enough to handle unexpected events. Digital calendars often come with helpful features like reminder alerts and color-coding for task segregation.

2. **Task Lists**: These can be simple to-do lists or more advanced forms like Eisenhower box (a four-quadrant box to segregate tasks based on importance and urgency) or the Kanban system (a workflow visualization tool).

3. **Time Trackers**: Time tracking apps can provide insightful data about how long tasks are taking and where your time is going. This data can help you optimize your schedule and recognize productivity patterns.

4. **Productivity Apps**: A plethora of productivity apps are available today that can help manage time effectively. From project management platforms like Trello and Asana to distraction-reducing apps like StayFocused and RescueTime, there are myriads of options to hold onto each valuable second.

5. **Ability to Prioritize**: Remember, not all tasks are created equal. Some tasks have higher importance or more pressing deadlines.

6. **Ability to Plan**: Having a clear, actionable plan helps streamline your day, reducing the possibility of being overwhelmed or wasting time on inefficient activities.

7. **Ability to Delegate**: The ability to delegate is an underutilized time management tool. Learning when to delegate allows you to focus on your top priorities.

8. **Ability to Say No**: Be aware of your capacity. Overcommitting is a guaranteed way to mismanage your time. Knowing when to say 'no' can help maintain productivity and reduce stress.

7.3. Time Management Strategies: The Essentials

Efficient time management extends itself beyond the possession and usage of tools. It's more about intelligent work and less about hard work. That means you need to have suitable strategies in place to ensure you're making the most effective use of your time. Here are some essential strategies:

1. **Prioritize Your Tasks**: Start your day by listing all tasks you need to complete and prioritize them based on importance and urgency using techniques such as the Eisenhower Matrix or the ABCDE method.

2. **Establish Clear Goals**: Having well-defined SMART (Specific, Measurable, Achievable, Relevant, Time-bound) goals can help direct your attention and energy towards productive activities.

3. **Block Time for Important Tasks**: Make sure to set aside dedicated blocks of time in your day for key tasks. It prevents scattering your attention and ensures quality output.

4. **Limit Multitasking**: Studies have shown that our brains are not designed well for dividing attention across multiple tasks. It can lead to errors and make tasks take longer.

5. **Break Down Large Tasks**: Break big tasks into smaller, manageable parts to avoid feeling overwhelmed, increasing the likelihood of successful completion.

6. **Take Regular Breaks**: Incorporate short, regular breaks into your schedule to stay mentally fresh. Techniques such as the Pomodoro Technique can be helpful.

7.4. Conclusion: The Journey to Mastery

Mastering time management is more of a journey than a destination. It requires embracing new habits, developing key skills, and continuously refining your strategies and techniques. As you get better at managing your time, you'll find it easier to stay on top of your tasks, reduce your stress levels, and create more time for the things you love. The journey might not be easy, but the rewards are plentiful. Embrace the process, and soon enough, you'll grow into a master of this critical life skill.

Chapter 8. The Art of Deep Work: Achieving Laser-Like Focus

Ideas drive progress and conceptualization turns potential into reality. Key to both are mental energy and focus, resources boundless in your brain's treasure chest. By understanding the principles of deep work, you can harness these resources, sharpen your focus, and supercharge your productivity.

8.1. Deep Work: The Concept

Deep work refers to professional activities performed in a state of distraction-free concentration. Here, your cognitive capabilities are pushed to their limits and value-adding output is created. This state results in skill refinement and scalable impact. By contrast, shallow work tasks, although necessary sometimes, don't require full cognitive attention and thus have limited value. The ability to perform deep work is becoming increasingly rare, but for those who master the art, it provides a considerable competitive advantage.

8.2. Identifying Deep and Shallow Work Tasks

The first step towards achieving laser-like focus is distinguishing between deep and shallow work tasks. As a rule of thumb, tasks that require intense concentration and contribute majorly towards our work goals qualify as deep work. These could include solving complicated problems, writing a report, or learning a new skill. On the other hand, tasks like answering emails, attending meetings, and handling administrative tasks constitute shallow work.

8.3. Cultivating Deep Work Habits

Cultivating deep work habits takes deliberate practice and patience. It requires shielding yourself from the flood of information that can fragment your attention. Begin by scheduling your day and allotting specific time slots for deep work. During these periods, minimize interruptions, be it physical, digital, or mental. This could mean turning off notifications, finding a quiet corner, or clearing your mind from extraneous thoughts.

8.4. Embracing Discomfort

Performing deep work requires you to embrace discomfort, particularly in an era of constant connectivity. When transitioning from constant interruptions to long periods of focused work, you might feel some initial discomfort, even anxiety. But remember, your mind is pliable and adaptable. Keep on track, and soon you'll find ease in this method of working.

8.5. Proper Periods of Rest

Downtime is crucial for productivity, as it replenishes mental energy and facilitates subconscious processing of complex problems. To cultivate deep work habits, it's crucial to take regular breaks for relaxation and allow for idle moments of contemplation. Respect your downtime, use it intentionally, and remember that rest isn't just a respite from productivity but a crucial part of it.

8.6. Creating a Distraction-Free Environment

A suitable environment is important for potency of deep work. One where interruptions are minimized and focus is facilitated. This could be a physical space—an office, a room in your house, a quiet coffee shop—or a virtual space. Tailor your environment to your needs—everyone's preferred work environment differs, and that's perfectly okay.

8.7. Ritualizing Deep Work

Develop rituals and routines around your deep work sessions to add a sense of predictability and remove the need for willpower. You could have a specific starting routine—a short meditation, setting intentions, or reviewing your task list. Similarly, wrap up your deep work sessions with a specific routine—like summarizing your work, stretching, or setting plans for the next session.

8.8. Embracing Boredom

In a world where entertainment is just a click away, boredom seems intolerable. But if you wish to master deep work, learning to embrace boredom is key. Resist the urge to fill every idle minute with technology. Instead, use these moments to let your mind wander, to daydream, this space for mental relaxation is crucial for nurturing deep work habits.

Achieving laser-like focus through deep work requires commitment, intention, and practice. As you nurture these habits, deep work will become part of your natural workflow, offering unparalleled professional progress and personal fulfillment. Remember, the road to routine deep work isn't a sprint, but a marathon that requires consistent and conscious effort. Dedicate yourself to the quest, and the rewards will be substantial.

Chapter 9. Optimizing Your Environment for Peak Performance

Your environment plays a pivotal role in how you perform. But how do you craft an environment that fosters peak performance? Here's the ultimate guide.

9.1. Assess Your Current Environment

Understanding your workspace as it stands is integral. Inspect your current setup - your desking system, the lighting, noise ambience, and colors around you. Note distractions and impacts they have on your productivity. Only when you understand what working conditions cause doldrums can you move towards optimization.

9.2. De-clutter Your Space

Clutter is debilitating. It breeds confusion, anxiety, and ineffectiveness. Give physical and digital de-cluttering utmost importance. Clear out irrelevant objects from your desk. Limit digital bombardment by smartly managing emails, avoiding excessive browser tabs, and organizing files in your digital workspace. The cleaner your space, the clearer your mind.

9.3. Harness the Power of Light

Lighting significantly impacts mood and energy levels. Natural light is ideal but if not feasible, opt for light fixtures and bulbs that mimic daylight. Avoid overly bright lights that induce eye strain and headaches. Appropriate lighting practices can boost productivity, increase energy levels and attenuate stress.

9.4. Invest in Ergonomic Furniture

Physical discomfort is a productivity-killer. Invest in ergonomically designed furniture ensuring your comfort. Adjustable height desks, chairs with proper lumbar support, footrests, wrist supports, etc., can make a tremendous difference in your working experience.

9.5. Establish Zones

Designate specific areas for specific tasks - such as designated space for brainstorming, relaxation, and focused work. This zoning approach gives your brain cues about how to behave in different areas, smoothening transitions between different tasks.

9.6. Manage Noise Levels

Find your noise comfort zone. Silence boosts creativity for some, while ambient noise like a coffee shop bustle improves focus for others. Experiment and find what works best for you. Noise-cancelling headphones can be a productive investment if you're easily distracted by audio stimuli.

9.7. Wall Colors : A Psychological Approach

Color psychology aids in productivity too. Choose colors that foster the emotions you want to cultivate. Blue stimulates the mind, yellow inspires creativity, red affects your body and green creates a calming balance. Consider your job requirements and paint accordingly.

9.8. Increase Natural Elements

Incorporate greenery and natural elements in your workspace. Scientifically known as biophilic design, studies show that natural elements can reduce stress, improve cognitive function, and enhance mood. Houseplants, nature-inspired artworks, and rocks can aid considerably in ensuring mental well-being.

9.9. Optimal Room Temperature

Temperature impacts productivity. A slightly chilly room improves accuracy of tasks, while a warmer room boosts creativity. Typically, aim for a room temperature between 20-25°C (68-77°F) for optimal productivity.

9.10. Adopt A Minimalist Approach

Embrace minimalism. The fewer the distractions, the better your focus. Keep only essentials. Removing superfluous elements creates a tranquil workspace that cultivates focus.

9.11. Control Odors

Bad odors are detrimental whereas pleasing scents improve mood and productivity. Essential oils diffused in your workspace can play a positive role in mental stimulation. Different scents can instigate various responses - lemon promotes concentration, lavender reduces stress, and peppermint lifts the mood.

9.12. Motivate with Visuals

Motivating visuals create a positive environment and inspire personal growth. Vision boards, motivational quotes, or images of your goals strategically placed, can serve as reminders of your objective and keep you propelled throughout the workload.

By adopting these strategies, you're effectively optimizing your environment for peak performance. Prepare to unveil a fresh wave of productivity as you fine-tune your workspace according to your needs and preferences. This is your path to a more energized, focused, and ultimately, more successful way of working. Be ready to embrace the remarkable improvement in productivity levels!

Chapter 10. Limitless Motivation: Sustaining High Energy and Focus

A promised land of peak performance and high productivity cannot be reached without a map and a compass, your motivation and focus. Welcome to the realm where high energy levels and laser focus are not just attainable but sustainable. In this chapter, we'll traverse the steps, strategies, and methods to fuel your motivation and sharpen your focus towards a state of uncharted potential.

10.1. Understanding Motivation, Energy and Focus

Before setting out on your journey, it is important to build a clear understanding of what motivation, energy, and focus mean and how they align. Motivation is the drive that pushes you to achieve your goals; energy fuels these efforts and focus directs your energy towards accomplishing specific objectives.

Motivation can be intrinsic or extrinsic; you might either be self-motivated or driven by external factors like recognition or rewards. Energy levels can broadly be influenced by physical health, emotional state and environmental factors. Focus is the ability to single out a task and steer clear of distractions. The harmony between motivation, energy, and focus is the foundation of extraordinary productivity.

10.2. Cultivate Habits for High Motivation

Motivation can be erratic, but habits have a remarkable ability to withstand the test of time. Cultivating habits that bolster your motivation is essential.

- **Set Clear Goals**: Visualize where you want to be and establish clear, achievable goals to guide your actions. Break down large goals into smaller ones to be less daunting and more manageable.

- **Celebrate Small Wins**: Regular reinforcement is an excellent motivator. Celebrating small victories can spur momentum to accomplish larger tasks.

- **Foster Positive Attitude**: Adopting a positive mindset can increase resilience and help maintain motivation during tough times.

10.3. Managing Energy

Understanding and managing your energy is key to productivity. Here's how:

- **Maintain a Healthy Lifestyle**: Balanced diet, regular exercise and adequate sleep can enhance your physical and mental stamina.

- **Energy Mapping**: Identify periods of your day when you're at your most active and schedule demanding tasks for those times.

10.4. Enhance Your Focus

Increasing your focus involves training the mind to concentrate on single tasks rather than multitask. There are multiple methods to enhance your focus:

- **Mindfulness and Meditation**: Practicing mindfulness can be incredibly beneficial in boosting concentration, reducing stress and improving productivity.

- **Technology Detox**: Periodically unplugging from digital distractions can help improve focus.

- **Healthy Work Environment**: A neat and positive work environment can lead to better focus and efficiency.

10.5. Sustaining High Motivation, Energy, and Focus

Sustaining high levels of motivation, energy, and focus may seem daunting, but with the right strategy, it is doable.

- **Understand Your 'Why'**: Knowing why you're doing what you're doing can be the most powerful motivation you have.

- **Adopt a Growth Mindset**: Embracing a mindset of growth and improvement can help maintain your motivation by seeing challenges as opportunities.

- **Build Strong Relationships**: Building supportive professional relationships can help keep you motivated and focused.

In conclusion, sustaining high energy and focus is not about sporadic bursts of productivity but developing and maintaining habits that foster a conducive mindset, optimizing energy levels and fostering single-minded focus. Embrace the strategies and methods discussed in this chapter, and you will be one step closer to tapping into your brain's hidden potential. Remember, extraordinary productivity is not only attainable, but with the right approach, it can be your new norm.

Chapter 11. Embracing a Supercharged Future: Next Steps to Maximized Productivity

The stage is all set for you to embrace a supercharged future, where every task is an opportunity and every day an adventure streaked with accomplishments. Harnessing the power of your mind will be an empowering journey, and these next steps will guide you on the path to maximized productivity.

11.1. The Mental Recharge: Coping with Energy Drains

Productivity isn't merely the product of time management. It roots from managing your mental energy. Just as your physical vigor ebbs with exertion, so does your mental energy. Recognize what drains you and develop strategies to cope.

Characterize your energy drainers. Jot down activities that leave you feeling empty, whether it's prior to, during, or post-completion. Often, these will be tasks that you actively avoid or dread. Once recognized, restorative strategies such as breaks, meditation, or listening to soothing music can be employed to reclaim lost energy.

Consider hiring, delegating or automating such activities. While some tasks are unavoidable, you could explore the idea of redistributing your workload. Delegate, if you can. Time saved from these activities can be better allocated to tasks that amplify your strengths.

11.2. The Mental Gym: Training your Brain for More

Just like a marathoner trains for the big race, your brain too needs to build its stamina for enhanced productivity.

Work on your brain's agility with exercises designed to stretch your mental capacities. Jigsaw puzzles, Sudoku, or memory-related activities can be a fun yet challenging start. Do not forget to increase the complexity over time to ensure continual growth.

Maintain a nutrient-packed diet with plenty of brain-boosters. Omega-3 fatty acids, antioxidants, and B vitamins could help improve your brain power. Stay hydrated. Research shows even slight dehydration can cause a drop in cognitive performance.

11.3. Digging Deeper: Annihilating Procrastination

Procrastination, like a power outage, can black out your productivity. Understand the undercurrents of your procrastination to elude its grip.

Acknowledge your distractions and confront them. Use strategies like the Pomodoro technique, whereby you focus solely on a task at hand for a stated period, then allow yourself a predetermined time for distractions.

Breakdown larger tasks into manageable ones. Start with easy tasks to create momentum, and you might just find the bigger ones aren't as daunting as they appeared.

11.4. Harnessing Your Peaks: Circadian Rhythms and Productivity

Everyone has high and low productive periods throughout the day, colloquially referred to as being "morning" or "night" people. This is ruled by our circadian rhythms, and understanding these can have a profound impact on productivity.

Map out your energy levels. Note down how you feel at different intervals and identify patterns of highs and lows. Schedule intense, high-focus tasks during your peak times and low-effort tasks during dips.

11.5. Embracing Technology: Maximizing efficiency through Apps

In this digital age, productivity apps are your allies. They can keep distractions at bay, help with time management, and aid project organization.

RescueTime is an intelligent app that provides insights into your daily habits, helping you identify how you're spending your time.

For task management, Wunderlist and Todoist can help organize and prioritize tasks.

Lastly, Headspace can assist in calming your mind through guided meditation, aiding in mental rejuvenation.

Adopt the habit of continuous learning. Like technology, productivity techniques are continually evolving. Stay abreast with the changing trends. Champion these changes and adapt as required for your continually evolving supercharged future.

11.6. Conclusion: The Ongoing Journey towards a Supercharged Future

Remember, the road to maximized productivity isn't a sprint, but a marathon. Hone your mental stamina, cultivate laser-like focus, and remain steadfast in the face of energy-draining tasks. Embrace the highs and lows of your circadian rhythms, befriend technology to drive efficiency, and never stop learning.

The journey beckons you towards an inspiring and energizing life where maximized productivity is the new normal. So step forth onto this exciting trail, and triumphant stories of exalting productivity shall be your everyday tale!